HUNGRY FOR GOD ...
STARVING FOR TIME

Five-Minute Devotions
for Busy Women

Lori Hatcher

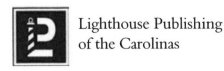

Lighthouse Publishing
of the Carolinas

PRAISE FOR *HUNGRY FOR GOD ... STARVING FOR TIME*

Lori writes as one who understands. She knows what it's like to struggle with questions, such as "God, how can I know if you really love me?" In each daily devotion, Lori addresses a common fear women face. She then provides insight from her own experiences, backed up by the truth of God's Word. *Hungry for God* provides a refreshing dose of spiritual nourishment for women who desire to grow in the Lord!

~ Kristen Feola
Author of *The Ultimate Guide to the Daniel Fast*

Lori Hatcher is a real woman for today's fast world. She knows life is lived between home and car, work and school. In the scramble, where is God? Like a trusted neighbor who knows when to stay and when to leave, Lori brings you to God through brief devotions you can use. Relevant, practical, and ideal for the Christian on the run, *Hungry for God ... Starving for Time* offers guidance from a writer who knows we all need divine help, sometimes in small doses.

~ Aida Rogers
Editor, *State of the Heart*

It's so important to me that despite the constant pressure to meet the demands of deadlines I daily face in the TV newsroom and community, I never lose sight of my main mission in life – ministry over media. Desiring to help others know Jesus personally and learn to grow in their faith requires me to keep my eyes on him consistently. A five-minute devotion to keep my focus sharp on our Savior is just what I need to fuel me through the rest of the day.

~ Dawndy Mercer Plank
WIS TV Evening Anchor

As a work-at-home mama wearing way too many hats to count, I need to be reminded that my many hats are blessings. I've spent years wishing I had a better quiet time, only to realize that for a season the Lord has given me four very non-quiet little girls. Lori's five-minute devotions are a perfect way to feed my soul and re-energize my spirit in the short windows of silence I find throughout the day.

~ Jenny Martin
Writer behind *SouthernSavers.com*

It's so easy to get caught up in our own small world that we miss the big picture. Lori invites us to take a look at life through the lens of God's perspective and holds out the "rope of hope" through Scripture.

~ Carmen Roberson
Veteran Bible Study Fellowship (BSF) Teaching Leader

Lori Hatcher has dropped a plumb line straight into God's most powerful messages to us, and delivered each one in a quick-byte format to spiritually nurture the woman on the go. Each five-minute devotion is candidly insightful and rich with relevance to the challenges facing today's busy woman. You'll quickly relate to the author's spunky humor and humility as she shares her own trials and resolutions. This book is going to be your dog-eared keeper.

~ Sue Duffy
Author of the *Red Returning* trilogy
and other suspense novels

Lori Hatcher is a truly gifted Christian woman, writer, and teacher. She is a blessing to all who interact with her, and now that she has put her heart in writing she offers the advantage of convenience. You can read these devotions whenever it suits your schedule. I enthusiastically recommend this book and know it will strengthen you for the day.

~ Dick Lincoln
Pastor, Shandon Baptist Church
Columbia, South Carolina

HUNGRY FOR GOD ... STARVING FOR TIME: FIVE-MINUTE
DEVOTIONS FOR BUSY WOMEN BY LORI HATCHER
Published by Straight Street Books, an imprint of Lighthouse Publishing of
the Carolinas
2333 Barton Oaks Dr., Raleigh, NC, 27614

ISBN 978-1-941103-82-1
Copyright © **2014** by Lori Hatcher
Cover design by Monique Nelson & Goran Tomic
Interior design by Reality Premedia Services Pvt. Ltd.,
www.realitypremedia.com

Available in print from your local bookstore, online, or from the publisher at:
www.lighthousepublishingofthecarolinas.com

For more information on this book and the author visit:
www.LoriHatcher.com

Brought to you by the creative team at
LighthousePublishingoftheCarolinas.com: Betty Hassler, Cindy Sproles,
Michele Creech, Meaghan Burnett and Brian Cross.

Library of Congress Cataloging-in-Publication Data
Hatcher, Lori
Hungry for God ... Starving for Time: Five-minute Devotions for Busy Women
/ Lori Hatcher / 1st ed.

Printed in the United States of America

Dedication

To my Lord and Savior, Jesus Christ

Many, O LORD *my God, are the wonders you have done. The things you planned for us no one can recount to you; were I to speak and tell of them, they would be too many to declare.*
Psalm 40:5

CONTENTS

Dedication...v

Acknowledgements.. viii

Introduction.. ix

The Day the Car Caught Fire 1

Bad Hair Days and the Kingdom of God............................5

Habits of the Rich..9

No Freedom of Speech..13

Sometimes I Wake Up Grumpy....................................17

Caesar, the 115-Pound Lap Dog 21

Eating Pocket Lint 25

Beautiful Eyes..29

I Quit! 33

Waiting —Torture or Treasure? 37

The Day I Missed a Miracle...................................41

Distressed or Damaged?..45

I's Wicked..49

My Latest Humiliation 53

Obedience Is in the Small Things 57

More Than We Bargained For....................................61

It's My Pleasure to Serve You.................................65

A Time to Be Served 69

Do You Tawk Funny? 73

What Would He Hear?..77

Living in a Glass House 81

An Inheritance from Grandma Eve 85

Green Bean Wars and Camel Knees 89

The Clock Is Ticking 93

Heavenly Arrivals...97

Blown Away 101

Making Sense of the Senseless 105

When This Sad,
Sick World Gets You Down...............................109

A Gift No One Returns......................................113

Does He REALLY Love Me?............................117

Hopeless in the Chocolate Factory...................121

How to Have a Relationship with Christ..........125

Endnotes 128

About the Author...130

Dear Reader 131

Acknowledgements

To every wise friend, Bible study leader, Sunday school teacher, author, speaker, and pastor who has taught me biblical truth, I dedicate this book. Thank you for speaking God's Word into my life.

To my writing mentor, editor, and friend Sue Duffy. You allowed me to sit at your feet and learn the craft. You believed in my potential, and you shared my vision for this book. Thank you.

To my editor and new friend Betty Hassler. You polished, spit-shined, and dressed my words in their Sunday best. Thank you for helping them put their best faces forward for God's glory.

To my daughters, Kristen and Mary Leigh; son-in-law, Josiah; and granddaughter, Lauren. *I thank God every time I remember you. In all my prayers for all of you, I always pray with joy because of your partnership in the gospel from the first day until now, being confident of this, that he who began a good work in you will carry it on to completion until the day of Christ Jesus. It is right for me to feel this way about all of you, since I have you in my heart* (Philippians 1:3-7).

To my husband, David. Thank you for supporting me, believing in me, and serving as my resident theologian. Your patience with my late night, middle-of-the-night, and early-morning bursts of inspiration is remarkable. Your willingness to let me go where God leads me and do what God tells me is a gift I don't take for granted. I love you very much.

Introduction

When I first became a Christian, I was hungry to learn about God but didn't know how to go about it. I remember buying an old Billy Graham discipleship book at a thrift store. Every morning during breakfast I'd read a short section, look up a few verses, and write my answers in the blanks.

I'm sure I got many answers wrong, but this fledgling attempt helped me learn about our amazing God. Thirty years later, I still spend time every morning growing in God's wisdom and grace. The devotions in this book are the result of asking him questions and searching for answers as I read his Word.

Each devotion begins with a question I call **Facetime**—something you'd love to ask God face to face, maybe over a cup of coffee. Some questions are weighty such as *God, this situation seems hopeless. Why even bother to pray?* Others are lighter, like *God, I'm having a bad hair day. How can I feel better about myself?* These questions offer a connecting point with God and feed you with his Truth. I hope my questions will resonate with you, and the answers I share will help you know God better.

To my Christian sisters who say, "Some days, I'm too busy for God!" this book is my gift to you. Between the demands of work, home, church activities, and family life, we're all stretched too thin, running too hard, and spiritually malnourished. We long to hear from God but just don't have time for leisurely reflection or hour-long Bible studies. Thankfully, though, even when we can't sit down to a five-course feast, even a quick nibble from God's Word can nourish and sustain us.

If you're hungry for God, but starving for time, these five-minute devotions are like a spiritual power bar—packed with spiritual nutrition—just what you need to get through the day. The book's small size fits perfectly in your purse, briefcase, or diaper bag. In the carpool line, at the kitchen table, or in the break room—just take it out when you find yourself with a few minutes between responsibilities.

It's my prayer that each devotion, selected with you in mind, will provide just what you need to grow in your relationship with God. And like physical food that satisfies us until we grow hungry again, I hope you'll come back to this little book again and again to be fed by the Father.

I'd love to continue to encourage you. You can visit me at my blog, *www.LoriHatcher.com* or drop me a note at *LoriAHatcher@gmail.com*.

The Day the Car Caught Fire

Facetime: God, life is scary.
How can I know you've got my back?

I didn't notice the smoke seeping from under the hood of my car until it drifted across my windshield.

Driving the interstate on my way to church one Wednesday night, I had one eye on the road and the other on the rearview mirror. My then three-year-old was entertaining her infant sister in the car seat beside her, and I was listening to their chatter.

Before long, however, enough smoke was coming from my engine to attract my notice.

FIRE! I thought silently, conscious of the tiny girls behind me. Images of explosive car blazes I'd seen on TV flooded my mind. Fear like birth pangs clutched hard at my gut. *I've got to get them out! Help me, Lord!*

Swerving hard to the right, I brought the car to a stop on the grassy shoulder. Cars whizzed past as I flung open first my door and then the door behind me.

"Unbuckle your seat belt," I barked to my toddler as my fingers fumbled with the clasp anchoring her sister's car seat. Swallowing the panic that rose like bile in my throat, I punched hard at the latch, and the buckle gave way.

Relief and fear caused me to jerk the car seat too hard, startling the baby as it slammed roughly against the doorframe. Her cry further frightened her wide-eyed sister, still struggling to unbuckle her belt.

Racing around the back of the car, I deposited my screaming infant on the grassy shoulder and turned back. My toddler's shrill wails pierced the night as she climbed unsteadily from her seat.

"Here Sweetie," I called, running toward her, but before

her foot touched the ground, strong arms scooped her up and deposited her safely in my arms. I sank on wobbly knees and clutched her hard. Tears of relief trickled down my cheeks.

I learned later that Mike, a long-haul truck driver, had seen the smoke oozing from beneath my hood even before I had. Not wanting to frighten the children with his horn, he silently pulled in behind my car and waited for me to notice the smoke. As soon as I pulled off the interstate, he followed. Jumping from his truck, he plucked my frightened daughter from the car and handed her to me.

Within minutes, the kind truck driver determined that steam, not smoke, was erupting from my engine, and my heart slowly returned to its normal rhythm.

Mike radioed his dispatcher, who ordered a tow truck. Once he was confident we were in good hands, he tipped his hat and was gone.

Often my life seems like that car ride. I'm cruising along happily until something goes up in smoke. And while I'd prefer to skip the drama, it doesn't always happen that way. This story provides an example of how God doesn't promise to spare us life's trials. He does, however, promise to care for us in the midst of them.

If my hose had split in the safety of my driveway, I never would have experienced his provision and care on the side of the interstate that night. He not only kept my children and me safe but also provided help when we needed it. We saw a living example of how God the Father cares for us.

I'm thankful that God, like my truck driver friend, has my back.

But now, this is what the LORD says ... "Fear not, for I have redeemed you; I have summoned you by name; you are mine. When you pass through the waters, I will be with you; and when you pass through the rivers, they will not sweep over you. When you walk through the fire, you will not be burned; the flames will not set you ablaze. For I am the LORD, your God, the Holy One of Israel, your Savior ... Since you are precious and honored in my sight, and because I love you." Isaiah 43:1-4

Bad Hair Days and the Kingdom of God

Facetime: God, sometimes I don't feel very attractive.
How should I handle these days?

As I prepare for a presentation, I begin praying far in advance. I pray for God to give me the message he wants me to share. I pray for every woman who will attend—that God will encourage and equip her. I pray for the event planners and ask the Lord to provide everything they need and give them wisdom and creativity. But on the actual morning of the event, I pray for something quite different—I pray for a good hair day.

Sometimes God answers *yes*, and sometimes *no*.

If you're completely honest, you've probably done the same thing. Tell the truth. Didn't you pray to be zit-free on your wedding day? Or bloat-free for your high school reunion? Or 10 pounds lighter for the family photo?

On important days, we often regress into bundles of adolescent insecurity. Having good hair, blemish-free complexions, or flat bellies doesn't make us into something we're not, but it does help us feel a little more confident.

So what should we do if, despite our best efforts, we have a bad hair day?

Remember that *man looks at the outward appearance, but the LORD looks at the heart* (1 Samuel 16:7). We can rest in the confidence that we are beloved and beautiful. Knowing that God thinks we're lovely because of what's inside our hearts, whether our locks lie down or let loose, should put smiles on our faces that are much more beautiful than our marvelous manes.

Don't *schlump*, as Mary Poppins would say. We should raise our chins, put on our best smiles, and look people in the eyes. Chances are we're the only ones who are aware of the cowlick that won't cooperate or the muffin top above our waistlines. However, if we act as though we wish we could crawl under the rug, even those who have no idea that our hair didn't turn out right are going to sense something's wrong. We need to put on our game faces and press on!

Concentrate on others. Before long, we'll forget we had a tussle with our tresses. When we take our eyes off ourselves and place them squarely on someone else, we gain perspective about what truly matters. Another benefit is that if we concentrate on helping others feel comfortable, confident, and cared for, this quality is what they will remember about us, not our crazy coiffure. Poet Maya Angelou agrees: "I've learned that people will forget what you said, people will forget what you did, but people will never forget how you made them feel."[1]

Remember that true beauty isn't determined by what our bodies look like, but by what our spirits look like. Peter wrote: *Your beauty should not come from outward adornment, such as braided hair and the wearing of gold jewelry and fine clothes. Instead, it should be that of your inner self, the unfading beauty of a gentle and quiet spirit, which is of great worth in God's sight* (1 Peter 3:3-4).

So tomorrow, whether it's a good hair day or a bad one, let's greet the world with a smile.

For you created my inmost being; you knit me together in my mother's womb. I praise you because I am fearfully and wonderfully made; your works are wonderful, I know that full well. Psalm 139:13-14

Habits of the Rich

Facetime: God, I want a strong faith. How do I develop it?

Sixty-seven percent of the wealthy watch 1 hour or less of TV every day versus 23 percent of the poor. Eighty-eight percent of the wealthy read 30 minutes or more each day for education or career reasons versus 2 percent of the poor. Only 6 percent of the wealthy watch reality TV versus 78 percent for the poor, and 81 percent of the wealthy maintain a to-do list versus 19 percent for the poor.[2]

Thomas Corley, a CPA, who wrote the book, *Rich Habits: the Daily Success Habits of Wealthy Individuals*, did extensive research to determine which habits rich people have in common. The results are insightful but not surprising. Habits, in large part, chart the direction of our lives.

I'm not particularly interested in being financially wealthy, although whenever I hear an appeal from a missionary, I wish I had the means to write every one of them a big, fat check. I do, however, greatly desire to be rich spiritually. I want to have an account full of answered prayers, six figures worth of kind deeds, and a nicely padded faith inheritance to leave my children.

Like Tom Corley's list of rich people's habits, there's also a list of spiritually rich people's habits.

Spiritually rich people spend time in God's Word versus spiritually poor people who spend time in man's books. Spiritually rich people invest time in prayer versus spiritually poor people who invest time in worrying. Spiritually rich people serve others versus spiritually poor people who serve themselves. Spiritually rich people invest their money in God's kingdom versus spiritually poor people who invest in their own kingdoms.

But these habits that chart the course of our journeys don't form themselves. We are not born with habits. "We have to form habits on the basis of the new life God has put into us,"[3] said theologian Oswald Chambers.

My daughter's swim coach always says, "Practice doesn't make perfect; practice makes permanent."

I'd like the habit of prayer to become so permanent in my life that it's the first thing I think of instead of the last. I'd like the habit of serving to become so permanent in my life that I volunteer spontaneously instead of needing to be asked. I'd like the habit of speaking words of affirmation to become so permanent that I no longer have to remind myself to build people up instead of tearing them down. Establishing these habits will make me rich spiritually, allowing me to store up a treasure of good works that will bring God glory.

Until these practices become permanent, however, I must intentionally discipline myself. All day long I face choices about how to spend my time, energy, and money. Every time I say *yes* to what God wants for me, and *no* to what my selfish nature desires, I am one step closer to building a permanent habit. And even after I establish my habits, I must remain diligent because, as the apostle Paul shared with agonizing transparency, *what I want to do I do not do, but what I hate I do* (Romans 7:15). I'm thankful that as I yield myself to God, he will empower me.

Do you want to be rich spiritually? Begin by building godly habits.

Which permanent habits would you like to build? How will you begin to practice them today?

Be imitators of God, therefore, as dearly loved children. Ephesians 5:1

No Freedom of Speech

Facetime: God, I can't believe she just said that to me!
Why shouldn't I respond the same way?

As we exited the Metro station in Washington, D.C., my daughter and I stumbled upon a crowd of 300 to 500 people huddled under umbrellas around a stage bigger than their gathering. In an article I saw later, *Huffington Post* reporter Kimberly Winston estimated 8,000 to 10,000 people attended the "Reason Rally" Largest Gathering of Nonbelievers.[4]

One of us miscounted.

As we made our way to the Tidal Basin that ringed the city, the voice of the rally's speaker carried clearly across the largely empty grassy area. I only had to listen for a moment to realize two things. First, he was angry. He was railing at people of faith—so angry in fact he was cursing them. I wondered, ironically, what power he felt he had in damning people in the name of a God he didn't believe in.

Second, as I observed the uniformed police officers with fierce looking canines encircling the staging area, I realized they were there not to censor his speech but to protect it. His right to speak—even hateful, damning speech—is guaranteed by the First Amendment to our Constitution.

This unsaved person was exercising a freedom I as a Christian do not have.

I can't curse those who don't believe as I do. I can't express hate or disdain for those who criticize what I hold dear. I can't outshout, bully, or taunt them. I can't exercise the liberty of free speech because I answer to a higher law.

I answer to the Word of God. Jesus told me, *bless those who curse you* (Matthew 5:44, NKJV), *speaking the truth in love* (Ephesians 4:15).

I can choose to say angry, bitter, destructive words to those who disagree with me, but should I? The love of God compels me to do otherwise.

James 3:17-18 reads, *But the wisdom that comes from heaven is first of all pure; then peace-loving, considerate, submissive, full of mercy and good fruit, impartial and sincere. Peacemakers who sow in peace reap a harvest of righteousness.*

That day, walking away from the "largest gathering of nonbelievers," I chose to exercise my God-given freedom of speech. I chose to pray for those who were despitefully using my fellow believers and me (Luke 6:28, NKJV).

And I did it out loud.

Do not let any unwholesome talk come out of your mouths, but only what is helpful for building others up according to their needs, that it may benefit those who listen. Ephesians 4:29

Sometimes I Wake Up Grumpy

Facetime: God, I'm not always pleasant to be around.
How can I change my mood?

You've heard the old saying, *sometimes I wake up grumpy, and sometimes I let him sleep?*

Often, I'm the one who wakes up grumpy.

Perhaps I didn't get enough sleep the night before, or a child awakened me several times. Maybe the eggplant parmigiana I ate for supper did somersaults in my stomach, disturbing my rest and souring my disposition. Perhaps I'm still dwelling on a hurt or offense from the day before, allowing it to fester in my subconscious all night. Maybe there's no good reason for why I wake up out of sorts and cranky.

What's a woman to do when she's the one who wakes up grumpy? Here are a few suggestions:

Choose to be *swift to hear* and *slow to speak* (James 1:19, NKJV). When I'm grouchy, I tend to give my mouth *carte blanche* to say whatever comes to mind. Usually it's complaining or critical, and I typically direct my comments at those closest to me. As soon as I recognize the stirrings of grumpiness, I ask the Lord to *set a guard ... over my mouth* (Psalm 141:3, NKJV).

Put on praise music. Although praise music seldom changes my circumstances, it directs my thoughts to God and his goodness. Once I get my eyes off myself and squarely focused on God, my mood often does a 180-degree turn. It's hard to be grumpy when I'm singing about God's love for me.

Capture every thought. Second Corinthians 10:5 encourages us to *take captive every thought to make it obedient to Christ.* When I capture my thoughts and compare them to the truth of God's Word, I often find they are false, deceptive, or destructive. Evaluating them in light of God's Word helps me discard them and exchange their damaging power for God's promises. If my thoughts tell me, *no use praying about that situation—it's hopeless*, I take this thought captive and compare it to the truth of Scripture. Jeremiah knew that nothing is too hard for God (Jeremiah. 32:17). I correct my wrong thinking and am filled with hope instead of despair.

Adopt an attitude of gratitude. On particularly bad days, or when circumstances seem overwhelming, I may find m y thankful list is very short. Sometimes I'm so discouraged that I think nothing good is happening in my life. During these times my thankful list begins with intangibles: *Lord, thank you for my salvation. Thank you that you gave us the Comforter, your Holy Spirit, who lives inside me. As my friend Kim Jackson says, Romans 8:28 is not a typo. All things DO work together for good.*

When I intentionally thank God for the good gifts that come from being his child, I find it almost impossible to maintain my sour disposition. Often I'll speak my thanksgiving aloud. Hearing the long list of good gifts God has given me is usually just what I need to restore my joy.

Remember that this world is not all there is. Some days the world is so yucky that it's hard to see past it. The apostle Paul, imprisoned, lonely, and spent for the gospel, penned these words: *I consider that our present sufferings are not worth comparing with the glory that will be revealed in us* (Romans 8:18). Our time on earth is a vapor compared to a future that awaits us in eternity.

Finally, brothers and sisters, whatever is true, whatever is noble, whatever is right, whatever is pure, whatever is lovely, whatever is admirable—if anything is excellent or praiseworthy—think about such things. Philippians 4:8

Caesar, the 115-Pound Lap Dog

Facetime: God, some days I don't feel very brave.
Do my wimpy ways disappoint you?

Caesar was impressive. The biggest Doberman Pinscher I've ever seen, his head was bigger than mine. Flatfooted, he stood three and a half feet tall, but on hind legs, he could easily rest his massive paws on his owner's shoulders. Weighing in at 115 pounds, Caesar made everyone who saw him stop in their tracks, and most backed up.

They didn't realize, however, that Caesar was an overgrown lap dog. My Bible study group often met in his owners' cozy study. After we'd take our places and open our books, Caesar would survey the room. Gazing longingly at the now-occupied couches, he'd position himself directly in front of someone with an open lap. Turning his beseeching brown eyes upon the chosen one, he'd gently lay his massive head in his or her lap and wait for the inevitable strokes his shiny black fur invited. Then he'd release a sigh that emanated from the depths of his doggie soul.

"He'd crawl into your lap if he could," his owner would say with a chuckle and shake of his head.

I see a lot of Caesar in me.

Sometimes I'm big and brave. My faith is strong, my vision clear, and my purpose unwavering. I pray mighty prayers, dream lofty dreams, and accomplish great things in the name of the Lord.

Other times, I just want to crawl up in God's lap and sigh. The world is too big. The problems are too heavy. My faith is too weak.

During times like these, I'm comforted by the knowledge that God sympathizes with my weaknesses (Hebrews 4:15, NKJV).

Isaiah 40:11 shows me the Father-heart of God: *He shall feed his flock like a shepherd: he shall gather the lambs with his arm, and carry them in his bosom, and shall gently lead those that are with young (KJV)*.

Jesus also demonstrated the heart of God. In Matthew 23:37 he said, *how often I have longed to gather your children together, as a hen gathers her chicks under her wings*.

On sad, scary, or wimpy days, I find comfort in knowing that I can crawl up into my Father's lap and rest there. He's willing to hold me close to his heart for as long as I need.

Like Caesar, at times I look big, brave, and bold. Other times I'm frail, weak, and frightened. Either way, God meets me where I am. As I rest quietly in his presence, he lays his mighty hand upon my head and something miraculous happens. Nothing changes in my situation, but as I rest in his presence, he fills me with hope, strength, and the ability to press on.

> *He tends his flock like a shepherd:*
> *He gathers the lambs in his arms*
> *and carries them close to his heart.*
> Isaiah 40:11

Eating Pocket Lint

*Facetime: God, deep down inside, I'm very selfish.
How can I learn to be more generous?*

Pocket lint tastes awful.

The incident started out innocently enough. I bought some jellybeans after Easter. They were hard to pass up at half price, even though as a dental hygienist, I seldom eat candy. (Note: chocolate isn't candy; it's a food group.)

Sitting at my computer, I had just poured a handful onto the table and tucked the bag away when I heard my daughter's footsteps.

In an instant, I was a stingy 10-year-old kid again, trying to hide my favorite candy from my sisters. I scooped up the handful of jellybeans and slid them into my pocket. I moved so fast they didn't even have time to stick to my sweaty palms. I gazed innocently into my blank computer screen as my daughter passed through on her way outside.

When the coast was clear, I pulled out the jellybeans and popped a few into my mouth. Proverbs 9:17 flashed through my mind:

> Stolen water is sweet;
> food eaten in secret is delicious!

Then I tasted the pocket lint. *Blech!* I spit those jellybeans out so fast the color was still on them. And so was the lint.

Shamed, I was instantly convicted of my selfishness and embarrassed by my actions. Jellybean selfishness is a relatively minor misdemeanor, but I knew it was a symptom of my heart's attitude.

When I act selfishly, I forget that everything good in my life comes from God and that he loves to give generously to his children (James 1:17). I forget that out of gratitude to God, I should follow his example and give generously to others. Scripture says when I choose to be generous, I will enjoy blessings that far exceed whatever selfish pleasure I can grab for myself.

Proverbs 11:25 reads:

A generous man will prosper;
whoever refreshes others will be refreshed.

I know this is true. On good days, when I share with an abundant hand, I receive more pleasure than if I'd kept the blessing for myself. Those with whom I share are usually grateful, and even if they're not, I know God smiles at me. His "thumbs up" is worth more than an Easter basket full of jellybeans.

I've also noticed that when I share liberally, blessings seem to circle back around to me. These blessings don't come when I give with ulterior motives because I can never manipulate God's blessings. But when I share from a grateful heart, God always takes care of me. Abundantly.

So what's it going to be? A few jellybeans heavily coated in pocket lint or God's gracious plenty, wrapped in a smile?

Give, and it will be given to you. A good measure, pressed down, shaken together and running over, will be poured into your lap. For with the measure you use, it will be measured to you. Luke 6:38

Beautiful Eyes

Facetime: God, some people look like they have it all together. Do they really need you?

I knew what my husband was going to say before he said it.

We had just spent a few hours with Whitney, our new neighbor, and her mom. I'd invited them to church, and they'd surprised me by coming. Wanting to get to know them better, we'd asked them to join us for pizza after the service.

I sat across from Whitney, a beautiful woman about my age. She has wide, tawny eyes with long lashes. Her teeth are straight and white. While we talked, I watched her, thinking again how attractive she was. That's how I knew what my husband was going to say before he said it.

"I was thinking about Whitney," he said later, and the little worm of jealousy and insecurity wiggled inside me. "I was watching her eyes—"

"She has very beautiful eyes," I acknowledged.

"—but they're not like yours," he said. "They don't smile."

My husband saw what I had missed that day. He echoed the observation of the old English proverb that says, "The eyes are the windows to the soul." Unlike me, he had looked past Whitney's outward beauty and peered into her heart, which had an empty place without Jesus.

When we encounter beautiful people, we easily forget that what we see on the outside doesn't always reflect what's on the inside. Hollywood actors and actresses may look happy, but their lives tell a different story. Our friends and neighbors may have nice homes, well-kept yards, and cute children, but when the door closes and the shades go down, they often struggle profoundly. Like Christians, they face marital problems, economic fears, and health issues. However, they lack the hope and confidence available to believers. Without an anchor, they risk capsizing on the stormy seas of 21st century life.

I hope that day over pizza was the first of many spiritual conversations we'll have with Whitney and her mom. I pray, in time, that Whitney will come to know Jesus personally as her Savior. Then she can experience joy in her heart that will be reflected in her eyes. And nothing makes a heart happier than knowing Christ as Savior.

Today I'm praying for Whitney. What about you? Who has God brought into your life that needs to experience the joy that only comes from knowing God? Not superficial happiness, but the deep-down-inside joy that only Jesus can give? Pray for them today, and then take a step toward building a relationship that will one day grant you the opportunity to share the reason for the hope that lies within you.

A happy heart makes the face cheerful. Proverbs 15:13

I Quit!

*Facetime: God, no one appreciates what I do.
Why shouldn't I quit?*

"That's it; I quit! I'm not doing this anymore. No one appreciates me. It's too hard. I pour my heart and soul into this, and all I get are complaints. Let someone else do it. Maybe they can do it better."

Be honest. Even if you haven't said these words aloud, you've thought them. Maybe even recently.

If you've served in ministry in any capacity, even if it's only within your immediate family, you've probably reached a point where you felt unappreciated, unsuccessful, or unwanted. You work long hours for little or no pay, deal kindly and patiently with difficult people, and produce something wonderful with a minimum of resources. All you get in return, it seems, is conflict, criticism, and more impossible tasks.

And so you're tempted to quit.

There's just one problem. Quitting a job is fairly easy. Quitting a calling is virtually impossible.

The apostle Peter tried.

He'd followed Jesus with all his heart. He'd believed his words, embraced his ministry, and left all to follow him. Then things got challenging. Those glorious days of traversing the countryside, listening to great sermons and witnessing all of those sensational miracles ended, and something went terribly wrong.

So Peter bailed. Turned his back. Threw in the towel. Took a hike.

He went back to what was safe and comfortable—to what he could do without thought, prayer, or preparation. He went fishing.

I'm sure, thought Peter, *if I could just go secular, all my problems would be over. People would appreciate me. They'd pay me for my work. I'd understand what's expected of me, and I could clock out at the end of the day and leave it all behind.*

I am going fishing (John 21:3, NKJV).

I did this recently—in my mind, of course. I hit a rough spot in ministry, and all of a sudden my day job looked awfully appealing. For almost a week, I wandered around in a major funk. Words of criticism played again and again in my subconscious like a CD with a skip. The enemy whispered suggestions that my life would be easier, happier, and more fulfilled if I bailed. Like Peter climbing back into his old fishing boat, I mentally climbed back into my non-ministry world and went fishing.

But Peter fished all night and caught nothing.

This is what we catch if we turn our backs on ministry and go fishing—nothing.

No one is challenged, encouraged, or equipped. No one learns from our examples or benefits from our prayers. The body of Christ suffers because we checked out.

"Simon son of John, do you love me?" ...

"Lord, you know that I love you." ...

"Feed my sheep" (John 21:17).

When we contemplate quitting, we should ponder Francis Chan's wise words: "Your greatest fear should not be fear of failure, but of succeeding at things in life that don't really matter."[5]

Ministry is hard, whether we're ministering to our own

family or to a church of hundreds. But if we know Christ as our Savior, ministry's not an option. It's a privilege.

"Lord, you know I love you."

"Then feed my sheep."

You therefore, my son, be strong in the grace that is in Christ Jesus ... Endure hardship as a good soldier of Jesus Christ. 2 Timothy 2:1, 3, NKJV

Waiting —Torture or Treasure?

Facetime: God, I hate waiting.
How can I make the time more productive?

A s I brought John back into the operatory and seated him in my dental chair, I held out my hands for his glasses and newspaper. "I'll set these over here on the counter for you," I told him.

"Be sure you give those back to me if you leave the room, and I have to wait," he said. "I hate waiting."

"I agree," I said emphatically, "there's nothing worse than being stuck somewhere with nothing to do. It's such a waste of time."

We commiserated on the torture of long waits in doctors' offices and drive-through lines, and then I introduced another thought.

"Often when I'm forced to wait somewhere," I told him, "I use that time to pray." Perhaps because I placed an X-ray holder into his mouth—or maybe because he had nothing to say—John didn't respond.

Not wasting time is a biblical principle. Ephesians 5:16 encourages us to be *redeeming the time, because the days are evil* (*NKJV*). One way we can redeem the time is to capture those potentially wasted moments when we're waiting. Instead of chafing at delays, we can look at them as opportunities to pray. In this way, we're multi-tasking.

We can wait to have our eyes checked and intercede for missionary friends in Spain. We can wait in line at the grocery store and pray for our children's health and safety. We can wait for the lady to slice our deli meat and pray for our husband's business. It's a win/win situation. We go about our daily duties and accomplish great things through the vehicle of prayer.

An additional benefit to praying while waiting is having less of a tendency to become impatient and irritable. Instead of feeling as though someone is wasting our time, we can choose to feel we've been given a gift—precious time in our busy day to talk to our heavenly Father on behalf of those we love.

I didn't have the opportunity to say all of this to John as he sat in the chair while I cleaned his teeth. I wondered, though, as he waited for me to finish, if he realized he had lots of time to pray.

I challenge you: the next time you're waiting, redeem the time through prayer. You'll be amazed at what you can accomplish.

... redeeming the time, because the days are evil. Ephesians 5:16, NKJV

The Day I Missed a Miracle

Facetime: God, this is hopeless.
Why should I even bother to pray?

She was a lovely lady with a voice that was sweet, winsome, and compelling. Of all the soloists at our church, she was my favorite. When she sang, the joy of God was so evident on her face that the song on her lips was merely an echo of what was in her heart.

My heart broke for her when our pastor announced she had been diagnosed with a cancer so rare no oncologist on the East Coast would treat her. Her only hope was a clinic in Texas, he explained, and she was leaving immediately. He invited us to join him in praying that God would do a miracle and spare her life.

When I heard his words, my heart sank. I knew she was going to die. The hopeless diagnosis and confirmation from the oncologists who wouldn't treat her sealed the inevitable in my heart.

Two years later she stood before our congregation cancer free and once again singing to the God who had healed her. She thanked everyone who had prayed for her. She was a living miracle.

And I had no part in it.

I missed being a part of her miracle because I had not prayed in faith for her healing. Instead of believing the God who asked Jeremiah, *I am the LORD, the God of all mankind. Is anything too hard for me* (Jeremiah 32:27)? I believed the doctors when they said she had no hope.

Instead of believing Jesus, who said, *"If you have faith as small as a mustard seed, you can say to this mountain, 'Move from here to there,' and it will move"* (Matthew 17:20), I believed statistics that said her cancer was too advanced.

Instead of believing the God who said, *Call to Me and I will answer you, and show you great and mighty things, which you do not know* (Jeremiah 33:3, NKJV), I believed the reports that said she was beyond healing.

Was God able to heal this sister in Christ without my prayers? Obviously. My lack of faith did not hinder him in the least. God was more than able to fulfill his purposes for her. This precious lady was not harmed in any way by my prayerlessness.

Of all the people involved in this scenario, I was the only loser. I had missed the chance to be part of a miracle. While I rejoiced in her healing and praised the God who had brought it about, I had no share in the victory because I had not believed.

I learned several powerful lessons that day.

I learned that nothing is impossible for God. That he delights in working through the faith-filled prayers of His children. That nothing is sweeter than the victory that comes after doing battle on our knees. That when we unite our hearts in prayer around a common goal, God unleashes his incredible power. And I learned that every prayer victory makes it easier to believe the next time.

I missed out on the chance to be part of a miracle that day, but I purposed in my heart that it would never happen again. Now, when someone invites me to pray, I say, "Yes!" with all my heart. Never again will I miss being part of a miracle.

I am the LORD, the God of all mankind. Is anything too hard for me? Jeremiah 32:27

Distressed or Damaged?

Facetime: God, the faith life is hard.
Where do I find strength when I feel beat up?

"Look at that!" I exclaimed to my daughter. "They're asking full price for that chest of drawers, and it's got dinks, scuffs, and chipped paint."

"Mom," she replied with a sigh, amazed at my ignorance. "It's supposed to look like that. It's distressed."

Apparently, distressed is the new furniture chic. It's stylish to have peeling paint, bare wood, and scuff marks. Back in the day, when our furniture looked like that, it was either time to paint or replace it—not stick a price tag on it and sell it for twice as much as we paid for it.

Sometimes I feel distressed.

Disappointments rub the color off, and hurts dink the edges of my life. The wear and tear of life dulls my finish, and the real—less shiny—me shows through. Sometimes, betrayal takes a chunk out of me.

"Is that distressed?" I asked as I studied a table with a splintered edge.

"No, that's not distressed," my daughter replied, "that's damaged."

Some days I feel damaged, too.

Life is hard. If anyone tells you otherwise, they're lying. But life without faith is even harder. Sometimes, faith is the only thing that makes sense. I cling to promises like Romans 8:28: *And we know that in all things God works for the good of those who love him, who have been called according to his purpose.*

And Philippians 1:6: *He who began a good work in you will carry it on to completion.*

And Exodus 14:13, Joshua 1:9, and Rev. 21:3-4:

Be strong and courageous ... for the LORD your God will be with you wherever you go.

Stand firm and you will see the deliverance the LORD will bring you today.

God himself will be with them and be their God. He will wipe every tear from their eyes. There will be no more death or mourning or crying or pain.

Faith tells me weeping endures for a night, but joy comes in the morning. Faith tells me Christ came to heal the brokenhearted. Faith tells me God uses prayer to accomplish his will in the world. Faith tells me distressed and damaged is not discarded and defeated.

If you're feeling distressed right now, I encourage you to approach God in prayer. Tell him how you feel. Be comforted by the knowledge that his shoulders are broad, and his arms are strong enough to carry you.

After you've shared your thoughts with him, allow him to speak to you through his Word. The book of Psalms is a comforting place for troubled and hurting souls. David, a man after God's own heart, penned many of the psalms during times of doubt and searching. Finally, in the words of a pastor friend, remember, "Christianity is less about holding on to God and more about God holding on to you."

God's care reminds us that distressed and damaged is not discarded and defeated. Perhaps the designers have it right— distressed can be beautiful.

He has made everything beautiful in its time. Ecclesiastes 3:11

I's Wicked

Facetime: God, I worry a lot. Is this trait part of my personality, or can I do something about it?

I f fretting were an Olympic sport, I'd own the gold medal.

Before I became a Christian, I fretted about what was happening, what might happen, what wasn't happening, and what should happen. I fretted about the present, the future, and the past.

"Fretting is wicked if you are a child of God," [6] said theologian Oswald Chambers.

"We imagine that a little anxiety and worry are an indication of how really wise we are," he explained, but "it is much more an indication of how really wicked we are." [7]

In Harriet Beecher Stowe's *Uncle Tom's Cabin*, Topsy had to reach a point of confession and repentance over this sin in her life. "I's wicked," she sobbed to Ms. Ophelia.

And I have to admit, I's wicked, too.

"Fretting springs from a determination to get our own way," [8] Chambers observes, and it's true. I'm confident that God is aware of my situation and able to act on my behalf. I'm just not sure his answer will fit my agenda. C. S. Lewis described it this way: "We're not necessarily doubting that God will do the best for us; we are wondering how painful the best will turn out to be." [9]

King Hezekiah faced a valid threat. Sennacherib, the King of Assyria, sent a letter threatening to destroy Israel. It was a valid threat—his armies had decimated all the surrounding nations—and now he had Israel in his sights. Instead of fretting, however, Hezekiah did what we should do when we're worried—he took it to God.

Hezekiah received the letter from the messengers and read it. Then he went up to the temple of the LORD and spread it out before the LORD. And Hezekiah prayed to the LORD: 'O LORD, God of Israel, enthroned between the cherubim, you alone are God over all the kingdoms of the earth. You have made heaven and earth. Give ear, LORD, and hear; open your eyes, LORD, and see; listen to the words Sennacherib has sent to ridicule the living God' (2 Kings 19:14-16).

Hezekiah's godly actions are a model for what we should do when we are tempted to fret:

1. Go to God.

2. Pour out our hearts to him.

3. Remind ourselves who God is.

4. Pray boldly, asking him to glorify himself by acting on our behalf.

5. Rest in confidence, believing that he will hear and answer our prayers.

6. Trust the answer.

When I compare my circumstances to Hezekiah's, I realize I have no basis for fretting. The God who delivered Hezekiah and the children of Israel is the same God who is eager to act on my behalf. When I trust him with problems far beyond my ability to solve, he is then free to come to my rescue.

How about you? Are you fretting about something? I challenge you to take it to God and leave it there.

In the morning, LORD, you hear my voice;
in the morning I lay my requests before you
and wait in expectation.
Psalm 5:3

My Latest Humiliation

Facetime: God, sometimes I'm very self-absorbed.
How can I become more aware of ways to help others?

She shamed me, this woman with the big smile and even bigger umbrella.

It all began in the checkout line at the grocery store. I made small talk with the cashier as she scanned my groceries and handed them off to the clean-cut bagger standing nearby. Thankful I didn't have to bag them myself, I scanned my card and tucked the receipt into my purse.

Rain had been falling all afternoon, and I was thankful to have my umbrella. As I left the store, I popped the handle and raised it over my head. I briefly considered sharing it with my bag boy, following closely behind me. But I dismissed the idea. Sharing an umbrella, I decided, should be reserved for close friends, spouses, and members of my immediate family. Not strangers. I didn't feel comfortable inviting this nice young man into my personal space. Nor did I feel comfortable inserting myself into his.

I plowed on ahead into the rain until a cheerful voice stopped me in my tracks.

"Here you go!" she said, the lady with the big smile. I turned to see her holding an even bigger umbrella over my bag boy's head. His grateful smile spoke volumes.

"I'm so sorry," I called out, substituting my umbrella canopy for hers when we reached my car. She vanished, leaving me to my embarrassment. The bag boy chattered good-naturedly, oblivious to my chagrin.

I pondered the experience later, still smarting from humiliation and regret. How often, I wondered, do I hesitate to serve someone, hindered by boundaries of my own making? How often do I see a physical, emotional, or spiritual need and fail to step up because it makes me uncomfortable? How many opportunities have I let slip by while I weighed the options of whether or not to obey the gentle nudge of the Holy Spirit?

Too many, I'm sure.

But I don't always stay safely in my comfort zone. Three weeks ago, I threw caution to the wind and asked a patient if I could pray for him and his upcoming surgery. Last week, I made a meal for a young woman newly released from the hospital and brought it to her doorstep, uninvited and unannounced. Just yesterday, I shared an example of a poor parenting decision I'd made in the hopes that another mom might learn from my mistake.

But today I was selfishly unaware of the needs of those around me.

Tomorrow when I awaken, the slate will be clean, and a new day will stretch before me. Rain or shine, I'll be ready to minister to someone in Jesus' name. Just as Jesus "went around doing good" (Acts 10:38), I'll remember that service to others is the best sacrifice to God I can make.

And do not forget to do good and to share with others, for with such sacrifices God is pleased. Hebrews 13:16

Obedience Is in the Small Things

Facetime: God, no one notices anyway.
Do the little acts of obedience really matter?

The cup on the side of the road didn't look important, but it was.

Walking my dog one morning, I noticed the carelessly discarded trash and walked right past it. As I did, the Holy Spirit said to my heart, *You should pick up the cup and put it in the next garbage can.* It was trash day, and every house in my neighborhood had a green roll cart by the side of the road. Instead of obeying God's voice, I kept walking. All the while, an internal dialogue was going on in my heart.

Lord, I said, *it's just a cup. Someone else will pick it up.*

The words of James 4:17 were simmering just under my consciousness, ready for the Holy Spirit's use: *If anyone, then, knows the good they ought to do and doesn't do it, it is sin for them.*

But Lord, I continued, knowing the words *but* and *Lord* should never be used in the same sentence. *I've already passed it. I'd have to turn around to go back and get it.* The Holy Spirit then reached into the back pocket of my mind, which he has the full freedom to plunder, and pulled out a memory.

Dr. Falwell used to pick up paper off the ground. The late Dr. Jerry Falwell, founder of Liberty University and pastor of Thomas Road Baptist Church, was a mighty man of God. Students tell of small acts of service they saw him do when he thought no one was watching. Picking stray pieces of paper off the ground was one of them.

If that mental picture wasn't enough, the Holy Spirit rummaged through my mind's concordance and gleefully presented his *coupe de grace,* Luke 16:10: *Whoever can be trusted with very little can also be trusted with much.*

OK, Lord. I surrendered. I turned around, walked back, picked up the cup, and threw it into the trashcan.

Henry Blackaby, in his devotional *Experiencing God Day by Day*, writes, "Your life is the sum of the responses you have made toward God ... Whenever the Lord speaks to you, it will require an adjustment to your life."

He contrasts the examples of the early disciples with that of the rich young ruler. "Why did God use Peter, James, and John so significantly to turn their world upside down?" he writes. "And why were others, like the rich young ruler, never heard from again? Choices! The disciples chose to believe, and their belief was proven by their obedience." [10]

On this particular morning, it was important that I pick up the cup off the side of the road—not for the sake of the litter quotient in my neighborhood but because the Lord told me to. If I train myself to recognize his voice, and quickly obey what he tells me to do, even a small, seemingly insignificant act like picking a piece of trash off the side of the road will prepare me to say *yes* when he calls me to do something big for him.

I want to be like Peter, James, John, and Dr. Falwell and do great things for God. I suspect you do too. I wonder, what small act of obedience God will call us to today?

Will we obey?

If anyone, then, knows the good they ought to do and doesn't do it, it is sin for them. James 4:17

More Than We Bargained For

Facetime: God, I never imagined this would happen.
How did I get here?

We got more than we bargained for at our daughter's dance recital. She was three—the epitome of cuteness. Dressed in baby blue and sequins and holding a lollypop, she and the rest of her beginning dance class tapped their way around a lopsided circle for their two-minute spot in the performance. It was a fun conclusion to her first semester of dance lessons.

What came next, however, wasn't fun or cute. As class after class took its place on stage, the music, costumes, and dances began to change. What began as simple and sweet gradually morphed into suggestive and sensual. By the end of the recital, the oldest girls, dressed in scanty leotards and heavy makeup, danced in ways that made my heart break and my husband turn away.

We withdrew our daughter from dance class the next day.

Proverbs 4:26 tells us to ponder the path of our feet.

When we caught a glimpse of what was down the road for our daughter if she continued in this program, we knew we didn't want to go there. Thankfully, we realized it before we were highly invested.

How often, though, do we find ourselves arriving somewhere we never intended to go? I believe this happens with everything from careers to credit card debt to extra-marital affairs.

If we stop to ponder the paths of our feet, would we:

Allow our children to participate in sports or activities that will ultimately consume our family time, dictate our schedules, and cause us to miss church on a regular basis?

Work closely with or enter into deeply personal conversations with a co-worker, church member, or friend of the opposite sex, thus opening the door for temptation and sin?

Purchase items (perhaps on credit) that will cost a lot to use and maintain, thereby limiting our ability to give to others when God prompts us? Purchasing what we can't afford also requires us to work overtime, nights, and weekends to pay for them, thus affecting our family lives, friendships, and church attendance.

Invest our limited time and energy in good causes while neglecting our families, homes, and churches?

Are you on a path you never intended to walk? If you pause, pray, and ponder the path of your feet, God, the giver of all wisdom (James 1:5) will help you choose what is best.

And it's never too late to turn around. I'm praying for you today.

Ponder the path of your feet. Proverbs 4:26, NKJV

It's My Pleasure to Serve You

Facetime: God, service with a smile isn't easy. Isn't becoming a Christian supposed to make my life easier?

Chick-fil-A® is the Cadillac of fast food restaurants. Its food is exceptional, and the dining rooms are clean and bright. What truly sets it apart, however, is the crew of smiling, respectful, hard-working people who wear their garnet and black uniforms. They provide better service than many sit-down restaurants, often coming out from behind the counter to greet customers, clear trays, and refresh drinks. Whether you order at the drive-through window or in the dining room, each employee responds in the same way, "It's my pleasure to serve you."

A lesson lies buried not too deeply under this pleasant statement—one we would do well to espouse. Chick-fil-A employees understand something Christians often miss—the privilege of service.

Chick-fil-A managers regularly remind their employees that if it weren't for the customer, they wouldn't have a job. This reminder helps each worker remember that the work they do is a privilege, not a curse.

I wonder how often we take the cursed approach regarding the lives we live for the Lord. If we encounter hardship, we whine about how God must not love us, or it wouldn't be so hard. When we're unappreciated or underappreciated, we consider quitting. When we experience conflict (often within our own families) because of our stands for truth, morality, and biblical principles, we're surprised and hurt. When we experience fear, health concerns, or financial struggles, we panic. We act as though God has never cared for us, and we have no basis for faith for the future.

Sometimes I'm a spiritual wimp and a whiner. When I realize the audacity of my complaint, the only appropriate response is to bow my head in shame. My weak-kneed fair-weather faith that wavers with the slightest wind of tribulation is the equivalent of saying to God, "You are not serving me well. I'd like to file a complaint."

How quickly we forget that he is the Master, and we are the servants. And he is the master who spared no expense, even his own Son, to redeem and rescue us. We have no basis on which to question his love.

I once heard the story of a man who sat down to a meager meal of bread and water. As he folded his hands and lifted his eyes heavenward, he said, "Oh God, you have given me bread, and water, and Jesus, too. Thank you."

When we take our eyes off ourselves and place them squarely on Christ, in whatever life situation or circumstance we find ourselves, we can say to the Lord, "It's my pleasure to serve you."

He who did not spare his own Son, but gave him up for us all— Romans 8:32

A Time to Be Served

Facetime: God, now I'm the one needing help.
Should I be stronger and just tough it out?

Accc ording to Galatians 6:5, each of us should carry his own load, and for the most part, we do. We live responsibly, work hard, and do without when necessary. We help, serve, and sacrifice to be contributing members of our families, churches, and communities.

On good days—strong, abundant, healthy days—we can carry our burdens and those of our sisters and brothers. It's the Christian way. The American Way. The responsible way. But on other days—days when, as fellow writer and speaker Tammy Whitehurst says, "life takes a bite out of your heart," or your health, or your finances, we can't serve others because we can't even serve ourselves.

On those days, we must bow our pride to the altar of need and say, "Help."

In this weak, needy, humble, broken place—we can't be givers. Or doers. Or servers. We must yield and be served. In God's infinite wisdom and grace, he's made provision for this time:

Carry each other's burdens, and in this way you will fulfill the law of Christ (Galatians 6:2).

Needing help is a beautiful, awful, pride-less, humble place to be. And it's a place where we can see God.

We see him in the hands that reach out to help us, the knees that bow to pray for us, the eyes that cry with us, and the easy, gentle words of the Savior: *"Come, all you who are weary and burdened, and I will give you rest"* (Matthew 11:28).

We're taught often and well how to give: generously, cheerfully, enthusiastically, wholeheartedly. We're not often taught how to receive: graciously, humbly, thankfully.

It was good for me to be afflicted
so that I might learn your decrees ...
I know, O LORD, that your laws are
righteous,
and in faithfulness you have
afflicted me.
May your unfailing love be my
comfort.
Psalm 119:71, 75-76

Whether we're in a serving time or a time to be served, a giving time or a time to be given to—we can rest in the knowledge that God has made provision, and God is here. We can accept the grace and goodness he offers and commit to glorify him in whatever state we find ourselves.

I know what it is to be in need, and I know what it is to have plenty. I have learned the secret of being content in any and every situation, whether well fed or hungry, whether living in plenty or in want. I can do everything through him who gives me strength.

Yet it was good of you to share in my troubles ... I am amply supplied, now that I have received from Epaphroditus the gifts you sent. They are a fragrant offering, an acceptable sacrifice, pleasing to God.

And my God will meet all your needs according to the riches of his glory in Christ Jesus. To our God and Father be glory for ever and ever. Amen. Philippians 4:12-14, 18-20

Do You Tawk Funny?

Facetime: God, I know my speech matters.
How can I use my words to reflect you better?

I used to *PAHK* the *CAH*. A Yankee transplant, I tawked funny. Plucked from the rocky shores of Narragansett Bay in Rhode Island and plunked into the Sandhills of Columbia, South Carolina, every time I opened my mouth, people knew I was "not from around here." There was no doubt about it.

In church last week, a soft-spoken woman with a gentle smile shared a prayer request, and I knew she wasn't from around here either. Her speech was lyrical and delightfully different. I found out later she had moved here from Europe as an army bride.

My daughter recently took a dialect test. Using a series of questions, it pinpointed which region of the country her speech most resembled. Despite the fact that she's lived in the South all her life, her dialect strongly reflected the language of New Englanders. This fact comes as no surprise since she's been surrounded by "Yankees" all her life.

Whether we've lived in the same town or moved 20 times, our speech should tell people that we're not from around here—that this world is not our home.

Peter and John were good examples of this principle. Although they were hometown boys, religious leaders immediately detected something different in their speech. It had little to do with how they spoke and everything to do with what they said.

"Salvation is found in no one else," Peter proclaimed, *"for there is no other name under heaven given to men by which we must be saved"* (Acts 4:12).

Peter and John had nothing within themselves to draw people to Christ. No seminary degree. No charisma or polish.

No eloquence or advanced speaker training. But people knew where they'd been and who had been their primary influence.

When they saw the courage of Peter and John and realized that they were unschooled, ordinary men, they were astonished and they took note that these men had been with Jesus (v. 13).

I've noticed on days when I take time to be with Jesus, my speech is more likely to reflect his nature. Although not foolproof, filling my mind and heart with his thoughts through Bible reading and prayer better enables me to speak words that are kind, true, edifying, and full of grace. In Matthew 12:35 Jesus said, *The good man brings good things out of the good stored up in him.*

Being with Jesus is the best way to fill my heart with good things. Then, when my heart overflows, what splashes out blesses others.

Can people tell from our speech that we've been with Jesus? If not, perhaps we need to spend a little more time with him.

Encourage one another and build each other up, just as in fact you are doing. 1 Thessalonians 5:11

What Would He Hear?

Facetime: God, I try to do the right thing.
Does it matter that my heart disagrees?

Woosha woosha woosha woosha. Woosha woosha woosha woosha.

It was one of my favorite parts of my monthly doctor's visit. Even before I felt pregnant, and certainly before I looked it, I'd raise my shirt and expose my non-existent belly so the doctor could listen to my baby's heartbeat. After a pause, the ultrasound device he used would begin its rhythmic sound projection, and I would smile.

"That's a good strong heartbeat on that little boy," my doctor would pronounce. A month later he'd listen again. "That little girl sounds like she's exercising in there," he'd say, completely oblivious to the fact that he'd just contradicted his earlier prediction. I realized that while the Doppler device was very helpful to confirm that my baby's heart was beating, it was almost useless as a gender diagnostic tool.

As I look back on those doctor visits, I think about my own heart. And yours. If someone listened to our hearts, what would he hear?

Would he hear the heartbeat of a person who is sold out to Jesus? Paul had one. He often referred to his love for God, whom he served with his whole heart (Romans. 1:9).

Would he hear a heart that is sensitive to God's conviction of sin? The Jews at Pentecost had one. *When the people heard this, they were cut to the heart and said to Peter and the other apostles, "Brothers, what shall we do?"* (Acts 2:37)

Would he hear a heart that is pure? Jesus said the pure of heart would see God (Matthew 5:8).

Would he hear a heart that deeply pondered the things of God? Mary had one. She *treasured up all these things and pondered them in her heart* (Luke 2:19).

Would he hear a heart willing to invest some of this world's resources to gather eternal ones? Jesus observed that *where your treasure is, there your heart will be also* (Matthew 6:21).

Would he hear a heart committed to peacemaking and unity? The believers of the early church were *one in heart and mind* (Acts 4:32).

Would he hear a heart that speaks with gentleness, kindness, goodness, and self-control? *For out of the abundance of the heart the mouth speaks* (Matthew 12:34, NKJV).

Would he hear a good and noble heart, eager to learn God's word, apply it, and let it work its way out through our lives? *But the seed on good soil stands for those with a noble and good heart, who hear the word, retain it, and by persevering produce a crop* (Luke 8:15).

Would he hear a heart that doesn't despair when difficulties come, but rests in whom it has believed? Those suffering for the gospel's sake had hearts like this. *Therefore we do not lose heart. Though outwardly we are wasting away, yet inwardly we are being renewed day by day* (2 Corinthians 4:16).

And finally, would he hear a heart so full of God's love that it bubbles out for all to hear? Paul encouraged the Ephesians to have this kind of heart, *speaking to one another with psalms, hymns, and songs from the Spirit. Sing and make music from your heart to the Lord* (Ephesians 5:19).

Let us draw near to God with a sincere heart and with the full assurance that faith brings, having our hearts sprinkled to cleanse us from a guilty conscience and having our bodies washed with pure water (Hebrews 10:22).

Above all else, guard your heart,
for everything you do flows from it.
Proverbs 4:23

Living in a Glass House

*Facetime: God, I try really hard, but sometimes I fail
miserably. Aren't your standards a little too high?*

I live in a glass house ... and so do you.

Hang around pastors' wives very long, and inevitably someone will make a comment about the difficulty of living in a "glass house." She's commenting on how hard we find it to live up to the higher standard of behavior a church or community expects from its spiritual leader and his family.

I hate to break it to you, but the pastor and his family aren't the only ones who live in a glass house. If you're a Christian, you do, too. And more than the community is watching you.

God watches.

> For your ways are in full view of the LORD,
> and he examines all your paths.
> Proverbs 5:21

Proverbs 15:3 echoes the fact:

> The eyes of the LORD are everywhere,
> keeping watch on the wicked and the good.

While we should care what others think of our behavior, what really matters is what God thinks about it. Leviticus 19:2 instructs us to *be holy, for I, the LORD your God, am holy.*

Holy. Wow.

How in the world am I going to live in a glass house with the holy, pure, spotless, perfect Lord of the universe peering down on me through my glass ceiling? This news is worse than Santa Claus! Remember: He sees you when you're sleeping. He knows when you're awake. He knows if you've been bad or good, so be good for goodness sake.

Thankfully, there's hope.

God wants us to be holy because his reputation depends on it. (After all, he's our Father, and kids should never bring shame on their parents.) Holiness is also good for us. If we obey God's instructions for righteous living, our lives will be better, cleaner, happier, safer, healthier, and more fulfilled.

God knows we're frail.

> As a father has compassion on his children,
> so the LORD has compassion on those who fear him;
> for he knows how we are formed,
> he remembers that we are dust.
> Psalm 103:13-14

He's given us the power to be holy. And the good news is, we don't have to try, fail, try harder, and fail again, in a never-ending cycle of frustration. Philippians 2:13 reminds us that *it is God who works in you to will and to act in order to fulfill his good purpose.*

As we yield ourselves to God and feed our spirits, letting the Word of Christ dwell in us richly (Colossians 3:16), God begins to change, mature, and make us holy.

God has the responsibility to grow us. We don't have to sweat to make it happen any more than a peach tree has to strain to bring forth peaches. Fruit comes as the tree matures.

So welcome to the glass house. It's a good place to live with God watching over us.

He (God) who began a good work in you will carry it on to completion. Philippians 1:6

An Inheritance from Grandma Eve

Facetime: God, sometimes I'm stubborn and balk at my husband's leadership. How can I become more submissive?

I was sitting in the hall awaiting test results when the office manager called me into her office. "I can check you out now," she said, motioning me forward.

"The nurse told me to wait here until she gave me the results of my bone density test," I explained.

"Oh, you don't have to wait," she said with a confident air. "I can tell you what they are. You have early osteoporosis."

"Really?" I said, taken aback. "How do you know that?"

"I can tell by looking at you," she said, "you're a skinny white woman."

Turns out this office manager-turned-prophet was right—I did have early osteoporosis. And the condition is most common in—you guessed it—skinny white women.

The people most likely to develop osteoporosis are Caucasian women with small bone frames. These three factors genetically predispose me to this condition.

Like osteoporosis, I have another genetic predisposition directly related to my gender—the propensity to usurp my husband's authority.

My great-great-great-great-great-great-great-grandmother Eve was the first to exhibit this tendency, and the gene has replicated itself faithfully since the beginning of time. Just like my mother's Portuguese/Italian ancestors passed on their dark hair and inability to speak without moving their hands, Eve has shared one of her most troublesome tendencies with me and the rest of our gender.

This willful condition manifests itself in many ways. Here are a few:

Our tendency to question our husbands' knowledge or experience.

Our tendency to assume that our way/perspective/insight is automatically correct.

Our tendency to disregard his input and do what we want anyway.

The good news? Recognizing our problem brings us one giant step closer to a solution. Or at least a plan of action.

When I found out I had osteoporosis, I didn't sell my bike, buy a padded suit, and subscribe to *Wheelchair Monthly*. Instead of resigning myself to "the inevitable," I got busy. I did some research and discovered what I could do to either slow, stop, or reverse the condition.

I can employ the same active approach to my predisposition willfully to disregard my husband's leadership. Instead of saying, "Oh well, that's just how I am ... " I can take conscious steps to change.

I can commit to:

Ask for my husband's advice and input instead of assuming I know what's best.

Acknowledge that while his perspective is often different from mine, it, too, is valuable and worth considering.

Listen fully to his thoughts and ideas, not just long enough to know which direction he's heading and formulate an argument against it.

When I went back to the doctor two years after my initial diagnosis, my bone density numbers had not only stopped decreasing but had actually risen. By taking active, positive steps, my prospect for long-term health improved dramatically.

I wish my prescription against the disease of willful independence worked as quickly. I suspect, like my tendency to talk with my hands, I'll have to work on it for the rest of my life. Thankfully, I can trust that as I yield my will to God, he'll continue to enable me to be a wise, respectful wife who honors my Savior as I honor my husband.

Submit to one another out of reverence for Christ. Ephesians 5:21

Green Bean Wars and Camel Knees

Facetime: God, I'm not seeing results.
Why should I keep praying?

I knew I could outlast 'em.

Normally easy going, my mother seldom forced us to eat food we didn't like. But that day she must have read the "5 Reasons Your Child Needs Green Beans" article in the latest *Parents Magazine*. Mom had always respected my aversion to green food, so the five slimy green beans she spooned onto my dinner plate puzzled me.

"I don't like green beans," I reminded her.

"Well, you can't leave the table unless you eat them," she responded, crossing her arms for emphasis.

Mealtime came and went. My other, more compliant, siblings choked down their required quota of beans and went out to play. Mom cleared the dinner table, washed the dishes, and still I sat, staring at my plate.

Considering my prospects, I noticed the longer the green beans sat there, the more shriveled they became. If I waited long enough, I reasoned, perhaps they would shrivel up completely and disappear. I would be emancipated.

I determined to outlast them.

After an hour of watching me from the other room, Mom stomped back into the kitchen where I sat and said with a huff, "Oh, go outside for heaven's sake!"

I had won the Green Bean War.

Many years later, when I began to learn about prayer, I encountered several inspiring examples of similarly stubborn persistence.

Jacob wrestled with the angel of God and declared, *"I will not let you go unless you bless me"* (Genesis 32:26).

The Syrophoenician woman of Mark 7 humbled herself, begging Jesus to heal her tiny, demon-possessed daughter. To test her perseverance and faith, he rebuffed her initial requests for help. But she loved her daughter. She recognized that Jesus was her only hope. Instead of pridefully responding to his testing, she continued to plead gently with him until he healed her daughter.

James, the half-brother of Jesus, was such a man of prayer that he earned the nickname Camel Knees because of the calluses he developed from kneeling.

When D.L. Moody became a believer, he began to pray for his friends. All but one was saved in his lifetime, and the last trusted Christ as his Savior three months after Moody died.

What are you wrestling with God about in prayer? A prodigal child? A medical miracle? An impossible financial situation? A broken marriage?

God's Word promises, *the effective, fervent prayer of a righteous (wo)man avails much* (James 5:16, change mine).

He reminds us *those who sow in tears shall reap in joy* (Psalm 126:5).

I encourage you to join Jacob, the Syrophonenician woman, D.L. Moody, and me in praying with tenacity and determination. Claim God's promises with boldness and faith. Like the green beans on my childhood plate, with the Lord's help, we can outlast 'em!

Let us not grow weary while doing good, for in due season we shall reap if we do not lose heart. Galatians 6:9

The Clock Is Ticking

Facetime: God, my time on earth is limited.
How can I reach out to the people around me?

They're different. Military families, that is.

I live near Fort Jackson, one of the largest basic training facilities in the country. For 28 years I've been lulled to sleep by the sound of machine gun fire in the distance. I'm so used to it that the only time I take notice is when a houseguest turns to me with widened eyes and asks, "Was that GUNFIRE?"

What I've never gotten used to, though, are the military families who live, work, and worship in my community. Without exception, they are the most engaged and involved temporary residents I've ever met.

They are initiators. They don't wait to be asked; they jump right in. They are energetic go-getters who are quick to extend a hand in greeting, invite a new friend over for coffee, or volunteer to help.

They realize their time here is limited, and they may be transferred with very little notice. They don't have time to sit around. They might miss too many opportunities if they are passive.

There's a lesson cloaked in the earth-toned camouflage these brave folks wear. As Christians, we're also here on temporary assignment. We could be transferred with little or no notice. We are wise to be mindful of our impermanence as we move through our daily lives. It should affect what we do:

Always be ready to testify of your faith. First Peter 3:15 tells us to *always be prepared to give an answer to everyone who asks you to give the reason for the hope that you have.* Opportunities to share a testimony, word of encouragement, or even the gospel don't come along every day, and we should be watching for them. If we don't intentionally look for opportunities, we often miss a chance to share our faith.

Always be ready to extend hospitality. Don't wait for someone else to take the first step. My military friends know if they sit around hoping someone will invite them out for coffee, for a play date, or to church, they might be waiting a long time. Instead, they find a friendly face and extend an invitation. As a result, they often develop deep friendships that last a lifetime. Hebrews 13:2 encourages, *do not forget to show hospitality to strangers, for by so doing some people have shown hospitality to angels without knowing it.*

Always be ready to live with no regrets. While this isn't entirely possible, knowing our lives are "just a vapor," helps keep our priorities straight. I think of life's brevity whenever I'm tempted to hold on stubbornly to a grudge or grievance. I ask myself, *if I died today, would this matter?* Most of the time the answer is *no.*

We are here on this earth on temporary assignment. Earth is not our final home. What we do determines much of what happens in the world to come, not just for ourselves, but for those around us.

What are you waiting for? Time is short. Eternity is long, and we have much to do in between. Will you join me in the kingdom work?

All these people were still living by faith when they died. They did not receive the things promised; they only saw them and welcomed them from a distance, admitting that they were foreigners and strangers on earth ... they were longing for a better country—a heavenly one. Therefore God is not ashamed to be called their God, for he has prepared a city for them. Hebrews 11:13, 16

Heavenly Arrivals

Facetime: God, sometimes I wonder what heaven is like.
Will I be happy there?

I've never been in a place where everyone was happy, but the Charlotte/Mecklenburg Airport on Thanksgiving Eve came pretty close.

Because I'd allowed extra travel time for traffic that never materialized, I arrived at the airport with almost an hour to spare before my daughter's flight arrived. I settled into a chair near the baggage claim area and observed reunion after reunion take place.

A young wife expectantly watched the escalator. Wiggling with anticipation beside her were her two daughters, one dressed in pilgrim garb and carrying a basket of dried corn, the other dressed as an Indian, complete with long dark braids and a beaded headband. They squealed and bounced in delight when they spotted their father. Stepping off the escalator, he wrapped his family in a happy hug.

Equally excited, but without the Thanksgiving costumes, stood a Hispanic family of nine chattering and pointing to the top of the escalator. They watched as each part of a body descended, until finally their tiny, gray-haired matriarch materialized. They moved as one to engulf her and carry her away with their laughter, kisses, and smiles.

A man about my age stood off to the side. He anxiously checked and rechecked the flight board, then his watch, then the moving stairs. When his college-aged son arrived, this father engulfed him in a bear hug, a teary smile splitting his face like a knife through watermelon. "It's been so long. I've missed you," the young man's father said. "Welcome home."

As I waited for my daughter to arrive, I wondered if this scene might be just a tiny glimpse of what heaven is like. Perhaps loved ones we haven't seen in many years are waiting eagerly, just beyond the gate, straining for a glimpse of our faces. Maybe they're bouncing up and down as they anticipate our arrival. I can picture them, like my Hispanic friends, gathered together, chattering eagerly about how good it will be when we're together again.

But the best part of all will be seeing our Father, first from a distance, and then, there before us, in all his glory. He'll wrap his mighty arms around us and engulf us in a hug that will last for eternity. And then he'll smile—a great big, face-splitting smile as he wipes our tears away.

"Welcome home," he'll say. "I've missed you."

And I heard a loud voice from the throne saying, "Look! God's dwelling place is now among the people, and he will dwell with them. They will be his people, and God himself will be with them and be their God. 'He will wipe every tear from their eyes. There will be no more death' or mourning or crying or pain, for the old order of things has passed away." Revelation 21:3-4

Blown Away

Facetime: God, being led by an invisible Holy Spirit is a little strange. How can I know he's speaking to me?

The average wind speed in South Carolina is between six and seven miles per hour—a gentle breeze. Recently, though, the wind roared. It descended upon us with a fury that rattled the windows, tossed the treetops, and flung lawn furniture aside like bowling pins after a strike. It came at night, which made its power especially impressive. Because we couldn't anticipate each gust, we could only hear the effects as we peered out into the darkness.

Jesus described the Holy Spirit as like the wind in his legendary conversation with Nicodemus. *"The wind blows wherever it pleases. You hear its sound, but you cannot tell where it comes from or where it is going,"* he said (John 3:8).

The Holy Spirit resembles wind in my life, as well. Sometimes his voice is the slightest whisper in my heart. It may be a prompt to do something kind for another person, write a note of encouragement, or make a phone call. Gentle but persistent, the thought will slip itself into my consciousness like the reminders my mother would give me to keep my elbows off the table or say "please" and "thank you."

If I'm not listening for this quiet voice of God, I can easily miss it in the noisy bustle of my life. I've learned to sit—still and intentional—at the close of my prayer time, inviting the Lord to speak his will to me. If I sense his prompting, I'll write down the idea that comes so I won't lose it when I move to the next task of my day. Yesterday, the Holy Spirit said, *Buy that marriage book for Molly; she's struggling.* On another occasion, he advised, *Send that email to Pat; she needs to know people are praying for her.* His ideas are always timely and useful.

At other times the Holy Spirit roars into my consciousness like the wind on a December day. It swoops across my life, leaving me stripped and buffeted, gasping for breath. His words point out sin in my life or something I've been unwilling to surrender, and I'm ashamed and convicted. Face to face with my own selfishness, laziness, or lack of faith, I curl up into a ball and weep, disappointed that I have failed my Lord.

Still other times the Holy Spirit's blast swoops into my life and gives me a glimpse of his power and majesty. I see through spirit eyes how mighty he is on my behalf, or how holy, or how magnificent. He enables me to see God on his throne, with thousands of angels crying, "Holy, Holy, Holy is the Lord!" and I am swept away. I find it much harder to miss these tornado encounters with the Spirit, but I'm sometimes guilty of worshiping the experience rather than the One who caused the experience. Remember that God reveals himself so we'll be better equipped to serve, believe in, and tell others about him.

Have you learned to recognize the Holy Spirit's voice in your life? The best way to develop this listening ear is to spend time in prayer and the Word every day. Keep in mind that when the Holy Spirit speaks, what you hear will always agree with the Bible. He cannot contradict himself.

So whether the Spirit whispers or roars today, I encourage you to be quick to obey. God has a plan, and he's inviting you to be a part of it.

But when he, the Spirit of truth, comes, he will guide you into all the truth. He will not speak on his own; he will speak only what he hears, and he will tell you what is yet to come. John 16:13

Making Sense of the Senseless

Facetime: God, I'm hurting here. Why have you allowed this to happen to me?

We all wonder why bad things enter our lives. A deep loss. A wayward child. A cancer diagnosis. A betrayal.

We wonder if these trials are punishment. Misdeeds come home to roost—just desserts for some long ago sin. And while God does judge unconfessed sin, and sin does have consequences, there's another reason trials drag their burning tentacles across our lives. God uses these experiences so we can minister to others in similar circumstances.

In his book, My Utmost for His Highest, Oswald Chambers said, "If you are going to be used by God, he will take you through a multitude of experiences that are not meant for you at all, they are meant to make you useful in His hands and to enable you to understand what transpires in other souls ..." [11]

The Apostle Paul said it, too. *Praise be to the God and Father of our Lord Jesus Christ, the Father of compassion and the God of all comfort, who comforts us in all our troubles, so that we can comfort those in any trouble with the comfort we ourselves receive from God* (2 Corinthians 1:3-4).

I'll never forget the day God used another suffering soul to minister grace to me. I was mourning. Not a physical death, but the death of a dream I had for one of my children. Overwhelmed by the reality of the situation, I couldn't see past it to find hope for the future. When I shared my heartbreak with this kind soul, she reached out her gentle hand and ministered to me.

"Let me tell you about my son," she said. And by sharing in the fellowship of my suffering through her suffering, she comforted me. She had no answers to offer other than the love of God, who loves our children more than we do. By sharing her story, she made herself vulnerable. She redeemed part of her own suffering by entering into mine. In doing so, she lifted the burden that seemed so overwhelming to me.

And when I wondered aloud if God was cruel to allow hardship to enter my life, she comforted me with this glimpse into God's heart:

> *For he does not willingly bring affliction*
> *or grief to anyone.*
> Lamentations 3:33

Since that turning point, God has been faithful to speak words of truth into my life, answer my prayers in remarkable ways, and bring beauty from ashes. He has restored my joy and strengthened my faith. Although I still struggle when bad things happen, God has shown me how he can use the lessons I learn to help someone else.

Now it's my turn to redeem my suffering by comforting someone whose heart is hurting. Will you risk vulnerability by sharing yours, as well?

For just as we share abundantly in the sufferings of Christ, so also our comfort abounds through Christ. 2 Corinthians 1:5

When This Sad, Sick World Gets You Down

Facetime: God, this world is so sick and broken. Where can I find hope?

I knew better than to click on the YouTube video of the cute puppy in the shelter. When my daughters lived at home, they'd run interference for me. "Don't watch that movie," they'd warn when a preview came on. Or they'd say, "It was a good movie, but Mom can't watch it."

They know I'm tenderhearted and have a tendency to carry images around in my mind for a long, long time. This sensitivity is why they try to protect me from sad animal stories, news reports about neglected children, and tales about the abused elderly.

But sometimes the stories still sneak by. I hear about broken marriages, natural disasters, and suicide bombers. Fighting church members, hungry toddlers, and drug addicted homeless people. Cancer-stricken friends, bankrupt small business owners, and wayward children.

And my heart breaks. It aches for every hurting soul that walks this broken world.

I know the answers—that sin has been wrapping its poisonous tentacles around our planet since Eve's sin in the garden, and no generation is exempt. That we are engaged in a cosmic battle between good and evil that won't be resolved until Christ returns. That people will continue to hurt, kill, and destroy each other until the Prince of Peace reigns over all.

And while all creation groans to split its death-stained exoskeleton and be clothed in the light and life of its original, sinless skin, we must endure a little while longer.

These eight life preservers of truth comfort me when I am overwhelmed, and I cling to them:

God never intended mankind to experience sickness, loss, and death. He created the world to be perfect (Genesis 1:31).

He weeps with us, and we share in his suffering (Romans 8:17).

Where sin increases, grace increases even more (Romans 5:20).

When the burdens get too heavy, we can cast our burdens on him, and he will sustain us (Psalm 55:22).

The Holy Spirit in us is more powerful than Satan's influence in the world (1 John 4:4).

Our sorrow won't last forever; one day we will laugh again (Psalm 30:5).

Our present troubles will one day bear eternal fruit (2 Corinthians 4:17).

Eternity is forever and will totally eclipse our present time of earthly sufferings (Romans 8:18).

And so we cry, crawl up into God's warm embrace, accept the grace he extends to us, and press on.

What truths from Scripture comfort you when you feel overwhelmed? I encourage you to think on them today.

> *Even to your old age and gray hairs*
> *I am he, I am he who will sustain you.*
> *I have made you and I will carry you;*
> *I will sustain you and I will rescue you.*
> Isaiah 46:4

A Gift No One Returns

Facetime: God, my friend has given up hope.
How can I help her regain it?

She gave me a gift I didn't know I needed.

I was living through a spiritual crisis—what St. John of the Cross called a "dark night of the soul." Each new day brought additional information, and none of it was good. The reality was grim, and the future—even worse. In the quiet of night, while my husband slept, my mind would race down a maze of dimly lit paths to a common destination—desolation. Paralyzed with *what ifs* and *now whats*, fear would clutch my heart. How many times can the same heart break, I wondered.

I was a shipwreck victim desperately treading water as the waves crashed over me. And then she threw me a bit of driftwood, this friend of mine. A victim of the same spiritual nor'easter, she didn't have a Coast Guard cutter or even an inflatable life raft. Just a plank. But I clung to it desperately, and it kept this drowning soul afloat until the seas calmed, and the sun shone again.

In the inky blackness, she gave me hope.

"Hope is the thing with feathers that perches in the soul, and sings the tune without the words, and never stops at all," [12] Emily Dickinson so eloquently penned, and it's true.

Even the Apostle Paul needed hope. *We despaired even of life*, he wrote to the Corinthian believers, his very words bleeding wet misery onto the pages. *We had the sentence of death in ourselves* (2 Corinthians 2:8-9, KJV).

When we are hopeless, our hearts hemorrhage. Hope is the tourniquet. It staunches the flow, holding the wound closed long enough for life's blood to clot and healing to begin.

Because my kind friend knew Christ, the God of all

hope, she spoke truth into my distorted perception of my circumstances.

Until the still small voice of hope whispered sweet truth.

If you'd like to follow her example, here are five ways we can be the voice of hope in someone else's life:

1. Pray for her and with her. Our prayers will unleash God's power and shore up a crumbling faith foundation. ... *you also helping together in prayer for us* (2 Corinthians 1:11).

2. Remind her how God has worked in the past and challenge her to trust him for the future. *He has delivered us from such a deadly peril, and he will deliver us again. On him we have set our hope that he will continue to deliver us* (2 Corinthians 1:10).

3. Remind her of the work God has done in her life, and encourage her to trust him to do the same in the lives of those she loves.

> *He lifted me out of the slimy pit,*
> *out of the mud and mire;*
> *he set my feet on a rock*
> *and gave me a firm place to stand.*
> Psalm 40:2

4. Point her to God's Word.

> *You are my hiding place;*
> *you will protect me from trouble*
> *and surround me with songs of deliverance.*
> Psalm 32:7

5. Remind her that nothing is impossible with God. Think of Abraham, who *against all hope ... believed and so became the father of many nations, just as it had been said to him* (Romans 4:18).

Whether we are the ones bestowing the precious gift of hope or the ones receiving it, we must never underestimate its power.

May the God of hope fill you with all joy and peace as you trust in him, so that you may overflow with hope by the power of the Holy Spirit. Romans 15:13

Does He REALLY Love Me?

*Facetime: God, sometimes I wonder if you really love me.
How can I know for sure?*

How do you know someone loves you?

Because they say they do? Talk is cheap. We all know those who talk one way and act another.

I'm afraid saying, "I love you," isn't enough. Fifty percent of marriages today begin with "I love you," and end—usually within the first seven years.

We know someone loves us by his or her actions. Actions trump words every time.

We've all heard the words, "God loves you." But does he?

Let's compare his words: *For God so loved the world* ... (John 3:16) with his actions: *He who did not spare his own Son, but gave him up for us all—how will he not also, along with him, graciously give us all things* (Romans 8:32)?

When circumstances cause us to doubt God's love for us, all we have to do is look to the cross. Looking at our day-to-day struggles against the backdrop of the cross means we can no longer doubt his love.

If God didn't withhold his precious, perfect Son, but allowed him—nay—appointed him to a torturous death on a criminal's cross for us, how can he not freely give us everything we need? Not everything we want (foolish that we are), but everything that he, in his infinite wisdom, knows we need to be conformed to his image and brought into a rich and full relationship with him.

Shame. On. Me. For *EVER* doubting his love.

He spilled the blood of his precious Son to buy my pardon, and I whine that he doesn't love me because I experience sorrow, disappointment, or hurt. I complain because interpersonal relationships are challenging, or money is tight. I doubt because my health fails, or my husband isn't always kind.

"There is no need to plead that the love of God shall fill our heart as though He were unwilling to fill us ..." Amy Carmichael says in her book *IF*. "Love is pressing round us on all sides like air. Cease to resist it and instantly love takes possession." [13]

God doesn't have to prove to me day after day that he loves me. I don't have to put God on trial every morning with ultimatums such as "Lord, if you love me, show me today. Help my children make me proud, let there be enough money in the checkbook, and have people treat me kindly. If you love me, prove it by making me happy."

God's love for me—and for you—was settled long ago. Once and for all. On a cruel Roman cross.

For God so loved the world that he gave his one and only Son ... (John 3:16).

Once we've settled the fact that God loves us, we can move forward into abundant life by resting in this glorious fact. Never again will we put God's love on trial. Never again will the winds of circumstance cause us to doubt. Never again will we crucify God anew, saying *Lord, if you loved me, you'd ...*

It's settled.

He who did not spare his own Son, but gave him up for us all—how will he not also, along with him, graciously give us all things? Romans 3:22

Hopeless in the Chocolate Factory

Facetime: God, how can I ever be good enough to have a relationship with you?

Remember the *I Love Lucy* episode when Lucy and Ethel were hired to work in a chocolate factory? Several unsuccessful assignments found them side-by-side on a conveyor belt in the Wrapping Room. "Your assignment," the drill sergeant supervisor barked out, "is to wrap each piece of chocolate and place it back on the conveyor belt. IF YOU MISS ONE PIECE OF CHOCOLATE," she threatened menacingly, "YOU'RE FIRED!"

She started the conveyor belt; the chocolate moved slowly down the line, and Lucy and Ethel began to wrap them. "Hey," Lucy said with a smile, "this is pretty easy." All seemed to be going well until the conveyor belt began to move faster, and they began to struggle to keep up. Before long, unable to maintain the pace, Lucy and Ethel stuffed chocolates into their hats, blouses, and, yes, even into their mouths. It was a futile and frustrating attempt at an impossible task.

I used to have a recurring dream that was very similar to Lucy and Ethel's workplace nightmare. At least once or twice a year, I'd awaken in a sweaty, heart-pounding panic, unable to remember what had frightened me. All that ever remained from my dream was the feeling of being incredibly overwhelmed. Whatever task or situation I encountered always left me profoundly hopeless and emotionally distraught.

Hebrews 7 describes this feeling of overwhelming futility in spiritual terms. The writer pictured the Old Testament priests making sacrifices over and over and over again, first for their own sins and then for the sins of the people. I can only imagine the priests, day after day, week after week, year after year, serving in the temple. They dedicated their lives to a futile attempt to expunge the sins of the people with the blood of goats and lambs.

I was condemned to a similar fate. Before I became a Christian, I began every day trying to be good enough to earn God's favor. Trying to do more good works than bad and perhaps tip the scales of atonement in my favor.

Resolutions, renewed determination, and times of confession did little to assuage the guilt and condemnation that hung over me as I pictured my works on God's scale. I could never do enough good to counteract my bad, even though I was a "pretty good person" by the world's standards. God's Word is true: *There is no one righteous, not even one* (Romans 3:10).

Ethel and Lucy, the Old Testament priests, and me— trying hard and never good enough.

Until one day someone shared with me the rest of the story:

Unlike the other high priests, he (Jesus) does not need to offer sacrifices day after day, first for his own sins, and then for the sins of the people. He sacrificed for their (our) sins once for all when he offered himself (Hebrews 7:27, parentheses mine).

When I acknowledged my helplessness and my need for a Savior, I exchanged the righteousness I could never attain for the righteousness God the Son attained for me. I was forgiven—saved *completely* (v. 25)—with absolute certainty.

I asked Christ to be my Savior in July of 1982. That summer marked the end of my old life and the beginning of my new. It also marked the end of the nightmares that had haunted me for years. I was free.

What about you? Are you trapped in a futile attempt to be good enough, to change, to live the life God wants for you? Or have you given up trying? Recognizing your helplessness is the first step on the path of salvation. If you'd like more information about how to have a relationship with Christ, please turn to the next page.

For it is by grace you have been saved, through faith—and this not from yourselves, it is the gift of God—not by works, so that no one can boast. Ephesians 2:8-9.

How to Have a Relationship with Christ

The Bible tells us how:

We must understand that we have sinned and our sin offends a holy God.

For all have sinned and fall short of the glory of God (Romans 3:23).

Because we are sinners, we are separated from God and deserve to die and spend eternity in hell.

For the wages of sin is death (Romans 6:23).

We can't do anything to earn our place in heaven.

For it is by grace you have been saved, through faith—and this is not from yourselves, it is the gift of God—not by works, so that no one can boast (Ephesians 2:8-9).

God loved us so much he sacrificed his sinless, perfect Son, Jesus, to pay for our sin.

For God so loved the world that he gave his one and only Son, that whoever believes in him shall not perish but have eternal life (John 3:16).

God made him who had no sin to be sin for us, so that in him we might become the righteousness of God (2 Corinthians 5:21).

We must be willing to repent (turn away) from our sin and accept by faith what Jesus did for us on the cross. When we do this, God promises us a relationship with him and a forever home in heaven.

... but the gift of God is eternal life in Christ Jesus our Lord (Romans 6:23).

If you want to have a relationship with God, tell him.

Here's a sample prayer:

"God, I know that I am a sinner who doesn't deserve a place in your heaven. Today I repent of my sin, and I surrender my life to you. I accept what Jesus did for me when he died on the cross. Come into my heart, God, and make me a new person."

If you prayed this prayer, or said the same thing in your own words and really meant it, God has something to say to you:

If you declare with your mouth, "Jesus is Lord," and believe in your heart that God raised him from the dead, you will be saved (Romans 10:9).

If you prayed this prayer, I want to rejoice with you and help you on your way. Please drop me an email at *LoriAHatcher@ gmail.com*. For more encouragement, visit my blog, *Hungry for God ... Starving for Time* at www.LoriHatcher.com.

If you'd like to hear my story on YouTube, please visit http://youtu.be/keMjNS1xuNA.

Endnotes

1. http://www.goodreads.com/quotes/5934-i-ve-learned-that-people-will-forget-what-you-said-people

2. http://www.daveramsey.com/blog/20-things-the-rich-do-every-day

3. Chambers, Oswald. *My Utmost for His Highest* (Dodd, Mead & Company: New York, 1935); 167.

4. Kimberly Winston, "Atheists Rally On National Mall; The 'Reason Rally' Largest Gathering Of Nonbelievers," http://www.huffingtonpost.com/2012/03/24/atheist-rally_n_1377443.html

5. Francis Chan, *Crazy Love: Overwhelmed by a Relentless God* (Colorado Springs: David C. Cook, 2013); 83.

6. Oswald Chambers, *My Utmost for His Highest* (New York: Dodd, Meade & Company, 1935); 186.

7. Ibid.

8. Ibid.

9. http://thinkexist.com/quotation/we-re_not_necessarily_doubting_that_god_will_do/158358.html

10. Henry T. Blackaby and Richard Blackaby, *Experiencing God Day by Day* (Nashville: B & H Publishing Group, 1998); 102.

11. Chambers, Oswald. *My Utmost for His Highest* (Dodd, Mead & Company: New York, 1935); 310.

12. http://www.online-literature.com/dickinson/827/

13. Amy Carmichael, *If* (online) steppinginthelight.com/wp-content/uploads/2013/03/if-amy-carmichael.pdf

About the Author

Lori Hatcher is a women's ministry speaker, author, blogger, minister's wife, and healthcare professional. She shares an empty nest in Columbia, South Carolina, with her husband David and their rescue dog, Winston.

Lori is the editor of South Carolina's *Reach Out, Columbia* magazine. A homeschool mom for 17 years, she's also the author of the devotional book *Joy in the Journey – Encouragement for Homeschooling Moms*. A frequent contributor to *Crosswalk.com*, her feature articles and devotions have been published by *Proverbs 31 Ministries*, *Mardel*, *Evangel*, *The Mother's Heart*, *Inspired Women*, and *Columbia Metropolitan Magazine*.

You'll find her pondering the marvelous and the mundane on her blog, *Hungry for God … Starving for Time* (www.LoriHatcher.com).

Contact Lori at LoriAHatcher@gmail.com.

Dear Reader,

As you complete this study, I hope you've found yourself even *hungrier for God* ... although perhaps still wishing for more time in your day.

I also hope you've been encouraged to raise a few of your own questions with God and found him eager to share from his abundant store of wisdom (James 1:5).

Writing can be a very one-sided conversation. If *Hungry for God* has blessed you, I'd love to hear from you. Would you drop me an email and tell me how? If it didn't live up to your expectations, I'd also like to know that. My email address is LoriAHatcher@gmail.com.

Finally, may I ask a favor? Every author knows that word of mouth is the best way to reach new readers. If others hear someone talking about a great book, or if they read a positive review on Amazon, they're more likely to purchase it.

If you're excited about *Hungry for God*, will you help me get the word out by posting a review on Amazon? Here's the link to my author page: http://www.amazon.com/Lori-Hatcher/e/B00AEYBJ4I/ref=ntt_athr_dp_pel_1. You can find all my books here. Simply click on *Hungry for God* to write a review.

Thanks so much for sharing your thoughts with me and telling others about your experience.

Gratefully,

Lori